I'm Saved! So, What's Next?

Mabel A. King

I'M SAVED! SO, WHAT'S NEXT!

Copyright © 2018 Mabel A. King

Published by Vision Directives & Mabel A. King

All rights to material in this book are reserved under

The United States Copyright Act.

All rights reserved. Printed in the United States of America. No part of this book may be used or reproduced in any manner whatsoever without written permission except in the case of brief quotations em- bodied in critical articles or reviews.

For information contact :

alexinia47@gmail.com

Book and Cover design by Minor Design Co.

First Edition: March 2019

ISBN : 9780578470702

All Scripture unless otherwise noted is found in

The Comparative Study Bible

King James Version

The Amplified Bible

New International Version

Copyright © 1965 by Zondervan Publishing House

TABLE OF CONTENTS

- **CHAPTER ONE** .... *PAGE 1*
  "THE THEN & THE NOW"

- **CHAPTER TWO** ………………………….….. *PAGE 16*
  "SPIRIT, SOUL, AND BODY"

- **CHAPTER THREE** …………………………... *PAGE 33*
  "PREPARING FOR BATTLE"

- **CHAPTER FOUR** ………………………….... *PAGE 41*
  "GUARDING YOUR MIND (SOUL)"

- **CHAPTER FIVE** …………………………..…. *PAGE 47*
  "DEFEATING THE ENEMY"

- **CHAPTER SIX** …………………………….…. *PAGE 56*
  "THE SEED AND HINDRANCES VS. FREEDOM TO GROW"

- **CHAPTER SEVEN** …………………….……. *PAGE 66*
  "FRUIT: NO FRUIT, FRUIT, MORE FRUIT, MUCH FRUIT"

- **CHAPTER EIGHT** ………………….………. *PAGE 79*
  "THE RESULTS"

- *NOTES | WORKS CITED | ABOUT THE AUTHOR*

PREFACE

"I'm Saved! So, What's Next?" is desisgned to enlighten believers as to the spiritual forces behind what they have been delivered from and the blessings that are theirs in the Kingdom of God that they have been birthed into.

This book will help to prepare believers for the challenges they will undoubtedly face and the victories that are theirs as they walk yielded to The Spirit of God working in and through their lives. It will unveil Jesus Christ and what He has already done for us. It will give each person to see what God's plan is for their lives so that He might be glorified!

Chapter 1
"The Then & The Now"

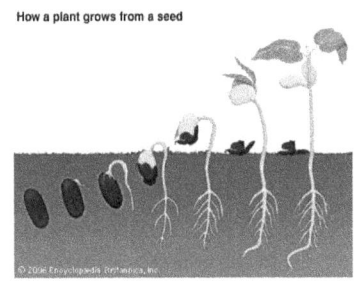

How a plant grows from a seed

Growth indicates that there is life, whether natural or spiritual. No growth, no life! Maturity, which is the results of growth, does not happen instantaneously. Growth indicates that certain levels of development have been met, but that doesn't mean that maturity has been reached. There may be other levels of development that need to be completed before maturity can be declared. What are the things that determine whether a person is mature or not? In this Christian walk, is it possible to be mature in one area and still immature in another? This study is designed to introduce you to your journey of growing up spiritually. You will discover that there may be no sudden, visible change, but if you will be consistent, trusting God to do His Work in and through you, inch by inch, step by step, you and others will be able to see your life transforming into the very image of Christ.

"The Then" – Before Christ

As you read and study, please keep in mind that when "man" is mentioned it refers to either man, woman, boy, or girl.

Let's begin. A person may present themselves as either, an unregenerate man, a carnal man, or a spiritual man. The unregenerate man has never accepted Jesus as Lord and Savior of his or her life. The carnal man has accepted Jesus as Lord and Savior and he has exercised enough faith to keep him out of hell, but not enough faith to live a godly life. The spiritual man has accepted Jesus as Lord and Savior and his or her soul purpose is to live a holy life that is pleasing to God.

Because of Adam's sin, we were all born into sin.

Romans 5:12 – *"Wherefore, as by one man sin entered into the world, and death by sin; and so death passed upon all men, for that all have sinned:"*

Sin is sin whether we did it to satisfy a carnal/fleshly desire, with or without the knowledge that God had forbidden us to do it or whether someone had trained us to do it from infancy throughout our lives, sin is still sin! Before Jesus came into our life, we may have found ourselves in one or more of the following positions.

Social Conditioning. Social conditioning takes place when our environment or those around us train us by word or through our observation of them, from infancy through childhood and beyond to have the same beliefs, behaviors, desires, and emotional reactions which they have or that are approved by them or by a certain group of people. These groups of people may have influenced us through any one or more of their traditions, prejudices, behaviors, our own friends, associates, church affiliations, or the media, etc. This was all we knew. It was what we were taught through what we saw them do or say. Even in the midst of all of this, The Word tells us that the grace of God that brings salvation has appeared unto all men:

Titus 2:11-12 – *"[11]For the grace of God that bringeth salvation hath appeared to all men, [12]Teaching us that, denying ungodliness and worldly lusts, we should live soberly, righteously, and godly, in this present world;"*

Before Christ came into our lives, we were influenced by our environment to sin, whether we were aware that what we were doing was sin or not. In the sight of God, sin is still sin. In many instances we did what we did because it was *"normal"* and that everybody else was doing it so it was the thing to do! We did what we did because we learned that this particular behavior was what it took to fit in, to be a part of the crowd, to be accepted, and to feel good no matter what we had to do. After all, it was our *"norm."* That *"norm"* could have affected the rest of our lives! But God so loved us and saved us!

Willful Sin, Spiritual Bondage or Strongholds. Before Christ came into our lives, we were sinning, may have been in spiritual bondage, and strongholds may have had their grip on our lives. That sinful, innate nature we were all born with as a result of Adam's sin just laid wait, dormant until a "trigger" awakened it.

Whether we ever committed a bad deed or not, we were still a sinner. Accepting Jesus as our Lord and Savior was and is the only way to be set free from a life of sin and from the penalty of death. That grace had appeared to us, to our conscience (Titus 2:11-12). But we had to accept God's grace.

Romans 5:12 – *"Wherefore, as by one man sin entered into the world, and death by sin; and so death passed upon all men, for that all have sinned:"*

Romans 7:18 – *"For I know that in me (that is, in my flesh,) dwelleth no good thing: for to will is present with me; but how to perform that which is good I find not."*

Ephesians 2:8-9 – *"⁸For by grace are ye saved through faith; and that not of yourselves: it is the gift of God: ⁹Not of works, lest any man should boast."*

Romans 10:9-10 – *"⁹That if thou shalt confess with thy mouth the Lord Jesus, and shalt believe in thine heart that God hath raised him from the dead, thou shalt be saved. ¹⁰For with the heart man believeth unto righteousness; and with the mouth confession is made unto salvation."*

Before Christ came into your life, you may have been oppressed or possessed by the devil. Times when you just couldn't stop doing something no matter how hard you tried. That thing just kept on pestering you until you did it, even when you may not have been thinking about doing it, but you just couldn't help but do it anyway. You just couldn't get any rest until you gave in. You just couldn't seem to get that thing out of your mind and it just kept on pushing you, and talking to you until you did it. But then, after it was all over, you thought you were free until the next time it came back!

Let's say, you were raised up in a so-called God-fearing Christian home, but you opened yourself up to demonic forces. You may have just wanted to see how drugs would make you feel. Or maybe you liked the feeling you got from alcohol, or you may have delved into the occult or sexually promiscuous behavior and couldn't break free, etc. You may have done it to fit in with the crowd and innocently opened yourself up to the devil.

Before Christ came into our life, and for whatever reason, sin and the devil had their grip on each one of us in its own way because of our innate, fleshly desires. Its claws were in us and we were held in bondage, held captive by the enemy until God saved us, until God delivered us! Thank God for Jesus!

"The Now" – After Christ

Redemption – Redemption took place when we accepted Jesus as Lord and Savior. We were redeemed from the curse of the Law which means that Jesus' sacrifice bought us back to God by His **dying in our place** on the cross and resurrecting from the dead in our place, and this is not based on anything that we have done. He did all this so that we might have **eternal life**! We have been **rescued, set free** by God through the shed Blood of Jesus. We are free from the sins that had held us captive. We are **set free from all the penalties** that were due as a result of our violation of the Law of God! Jesus did it all, forever, once and for all!

I Corinthians 1:30 – *"But of him are ye in Christ Jesus, who of God is made unto us wisdom, and righteousness, and sanctification, and redemption:"*

Galatians 3:13 – *"Christ hath redeemed us from the curse of the law, being made a curse for us: for it is written, Cursed is every one that hangeth on a tree:"*

Colossians 1:13 – *"Who has delivered us from the power of darkness, and hath translated us into the kingdom of his dear Son:"*

Acts 26:18 – *"To open their eyes, and to turn them from darkness to light, and from the power of Satan unto God, that they may receive forgiveness of sins, and inheritance among them which are sanctified by faith that is in me."*

Romans 5:19 – *"For as by one man's disobedience many were made sinners, so by the obedience of one shall many be made righteous."*

Romans 8:1-4 – *"¹There is therefore now no condemnation to them which are in Christ Jesus, who walk not after the flesh, but after the Spirit. ²For the law of the Spirit of life in Christ Jesus hath made me free from the law of sin and death. ³For what the law could not do, in that it was weak through the flesh, God sending his own Son in the likeness of sinful flesh, and for sin, condemned sin in the flesh: ⁴That the righteousness of the law might be fulfilled in us, who walk not after the flesh, but after the Spirit."*

Year after year sacrifices were made unto God, but those sacrifices never took away, never erased the sins of man! Only the Blood of Jesus, the Perfect Lamb of God was able to do that! We are now entitled to all the blessings found in Deuteronomy 28:1-14. You will find all of the curses in Deuteronomy 28 as well, verses 15-68.

1. Jesus said, "It is finished!" He completed what He was sent to do (John 19:30). The work is already done and we must accept it by faith!

2. All sins are forgiven—past, present, and future sins are forever nailed to the cross. When God looks at us, He sees the Blood of Jesus covering us!
3. We are delivered out of satan's dominion and authority!
4. We are born again! We are saved! We have been set free!

John 3:7-8, v16 – *"⁷Marvel not that I said unto thee, Ye must be born again. ⁸The wind bloweth where it listeth, and thou hearest the sound thereof, but canst not tell whence it cometh, and whither it goeth: so is every one that is born of the Spirit…. ¹⁶For God so loved the world, that he gave his only begotten Son, that whosoever believeth in him should not perish, but have everlasting life."*

John 17:3 – *"And this is life eternal, that they might know thee the only true God, and Jesus Christ, whom thou hast sent."*

Ephesians 2:8-9 – *"⁸For by grace are ye saved through faith; and that not of yourselves: it is a gift of God: ⁹<u>Not of works</u>, lest any man should boast."*

Note that good works didn't save us and never will! All the good works in the world couldn't save us! God's Grace saved us! We are saved **unto** good works (Ephesians 2:10). In other words, because of the Grace of God we are saved and because we are saved, God produces the good works through us as we submit ourselves to Him in obedience.

2 Corinthians 5:17, v21 – "[17]Therefore if any man be in Christ Jesus, he is a new creature: old things are passed away; behold, all things are become new.... [21]For he hath made him to be sin for us, who knew no sin; that we might be made the righteousness of God in him."

As a result of redemption, our ***spirit man*** was made new when we accepted Jesus as our Lord and Savior. We were crucified with Christ and rose with Him in resurrection to newness of life!

Galatians 2:20 – *"I am crucified with Christ: nevertheless I live; yet not I, but Christ liveth in me: and the life which I now live in the flesh I live by the faith of the Son of God, who loved me, and gave himself for me."*

Romans 6:4 – *"Therefore we are buried with him by baptism into death: that like as Christ was raised up from the dead by the glory of the Father, even so we also should walk in newness of life."*

In order to grow the way God would have us grow, we must allow the Holy Spirit to keep our flesh crucified by His Grace.

Now we have a right to all the promises of God to us found in the Bible. These promises continue throughout our lives as we grow in grace and in the knowledge of our Lord and Savior Jesus Christ. They are great and precious promises:

2 Peter 1:2-4 – *"²Grace and peace be multiplied unto you **through the knowledge of God, and of Jesus our Lord,** ³According as his divine power hath given unto us **all things that pertain unto life and godliness, through the knowledge of him** that hath called us to glory and virtue: ⁴Whereby **are given unto us exceeding great and precious promises: that by these ye might be partakers of the divine nature,** having escaped the corruption that is in the world through lust."*

Make no mistake about it, what you don't know ***can*** hurt you! The following are just some of the blessings listed in The Word of God that were ***given*** to us when we received salvation. But you must know that they are yours and ***believe*** that you have a right to them:

1. Soundness of mind – (2 Timothy 1:7; I Corinthians 2:16)
2. Health – (I Peter 2:24; Matthew 8;17; Acts 10:38 ***all were healed***)
3. Prosperity – (3 John 2; Psalm 84:11; Joshua 1:8)
4. Peace – (Isaiah 26:3; Isaiah 32:17; Philippians 4:6-9)
5. Deliverance – (Isaiah 54:7; Psalm 34:17,19; Psalm 91:15; 2 Timothy 4:11; John 8:36; Galatians 5:1)

Get to know those Scriptures that are promises to you or are connected to the things that God says about you. These promises are those that say, "in Christ," "in Him," "through Him," and "with Him," etc.

The Baptism in the Holy Spirit or Holy Ghost is a promise from God to us. (Note: The Holy Spirit and The Holy Ghost are the same Person.)

John 14:26 – *"But the Comforter, which is the Holy Ghost, whom the Father will send in my name, he shall teach you all things, and bring all things to your remembrance, whatsoever I have said unto you."*

Acts 1:8 – *"But ye shall receive power, after that the Holy Ghost is come upon you: and ye shall be witnesses unto me both in Jerusalem, and in all Judaea, and in Samaria, and unto the uttermost part of the earth."*

Acts 2:4 – *"And they were **all** filled with the Holy Ghost, and began to speak with other tongues, as the Spirit gave them utterance."*

Galatians 4:6 – *"And because we are sons, God hath sent forth the **Spirit of his Son** into your hearts, crying, Abba, Father."*

Have you received the Baptism in the Holy Spirit with the evidence of speaking in tongues since you believed? Speaking in tongues is the evidence or sign that you have been baptized in The Holy Spirit (I Corinthians 14:22). We need **_all_** we are promised by God.

The Word of God tells us that when we are baptized in The Holy Spirit we will receive power:

Acts 1:8 – *"But ye shall receive power after that the Holy Ghost is come upon you: and ye shall be witnesses unto me both in Jerusalem, and in all Judaea, and in Samaria, and unto the uttermost part of the earth."*

This power will help us in our **worship, witnessing, working** in the Ministry, **walking** out everything God wants for our lives, and to **war** (pray) in The Spirit! Sometimes we don't know what or how to pray for some things. That's when The Holy Ghost prays through us as we allow Him to, in words that we may not understand (Romans 8:26). We can do nothing without the help of The Holy Ghost!

Receiving the Baptism in The Holy Spirit

Any believer who has accepted Jesus as their Lord and Savior can receive the infilling of The Holy Spirit with the evidence of speaking in tongues.
Salvation is the only condition for receiving The Holy Spirit.
(Romans 10:9-10; Acts 19:2-6)

The Holy Spirit has already been given. All you will need to do is receive Him. He is a Person, not a "thing." Not something spooky. The Holy Spirit is just that, HOLY! (Luke 24:49, Acts 1:4-5, Acts 2:4)

You are not responsible for filling yourself and neither is anyone else. God is responsible and He will fill you with His Spirit! (Acts 10:44-46)

You must believe that you will receive The Holy Spirit. The Holy Spirit is received by faith just as you received Jesus into your heart by faith. (Acts 19:2-6) Just ask The Father to fill you with His Spirit with the evidence of speaking in tongues, believe and receive Him.

Any Spirit-filled believer can lay hands on you to receive The Holy Spirit, but hands don't always have to be laid on you. (Acts 2:4; Acts 10:44-46) Hands are laid on you as a means of agreeing with you that you will receive Him (Matthew 18:19-20).

You must expect to receive and speak. Not only must you believe that you will receive The Holy Spirit, but you must believe that you will speak with other tongues—in a new, heavenly language (John 7:38-39). Just as you would use your vocal chords, tongue, teeth, lips to speak English or any other foreign language, you must open your mouth and speak the new language that you have never heard or learned before. That language will be heard coming from the inside of you. It will sound as though you are thinking it, but it is a language you have never heard before. Speak what you hear, NOT English or other national language on this earth!

God will not give you something false, so don't be afraid. (Luke 11:11-13; 2 Timothy 1:7) God knows your heart. If you have accepted Jesus Christ as your Lord and Savior, have a sincere desire to be filled with the Spirit, and have asked God to fill you with His Spirit with the evidence of speaking in tongues, He will.

Forget your surroundings and speak. It's about you and your Father God. Praise God with your prayer language! Thank Him for His Goodness with your prayer language! You don't always have to be in church to speak. You can speak at home, in your car, etc. But the Holy Spirit will not act unbecomingly in public.

If you have never received the baptism in The Holy Spirit with the evidence of speaking in tongues, take some time now and receive the Holy Spirit by faith just as you received Jesus into your heart by faith. You may repeat this prayer:

"Father God, I thank You for saving me. Just as I received Jesus as my Lord and Savior by faith, I now receive Your Holy Spirit with the evidence of speaking in tongues. Thank You."

Remember, you must open your mouth and speak what you hear on the inside of you that is a language that you have never learned.

When you speak in tongues, you are praying to God. The devil does not know what you are praying. You can talk to God in your prayer language about anything that concerns you or others. You are praying God's perfect will down on your life and on the lives of the others for whom you pray.

Trust the Holy Spirit to do any work that needs to be done in you or through you! He is our Helper! He is our Keeper! He will keep whatever we trust Him to keep! Ask God to keep your spirit, soul, and body. He will!

2 Timothy 1:12b – *"...for I know whom I have believed, and am persuaded that he is able to keep that which I have committed unto him against that day."*

Chapter 2
"Spirit, Soul, and Body"

"^{26}And God said, Let us make man in our image, after our likeness: and let them have dominion over the fish of the sea, and over the fowl of the air, and over the cattle, and over all the earth, and over every creeping thing that creepeth upon the earth. ^{27}So God created man in his own image, in the image of God created he him; male and female created he them." (Genesis 1:26-27)

John 4:24 tells us that God is a Spirit. Based on what God said in Genesis and what Jesus said in John 4:24, we are made in the likeness of God and it is impossible for God to lie. Which means that *we* are a spirit. The **"real me"** is a spirit! The **"real you"** is a spirit!

Have you accepted Jesus Christ as Lord and Savior? Do you know beyond a shadow of doubt that you would go to Heaven right now if you were to die? The answer should be "Yes" if you have accepted Jesus as your Lord and Savior. This is why:

***Romans 10:9-10** – "⁹That if thou shalt **confess with thy mouth** the Lord Jesus, and shalt **believe in thine heart** that God hath raised him from the dead, thou shalt be saved. ¹⁰For with the heart man believeth unto righteousness; and with the mouth confession is made unto salvation."*

You confessed with your mouth that Jesus is Lord and believed in your heart that God raised Him from the dead. You are saved and have eternal life!

***John 17:3** – "And this is life eternal, that they might know thee the only true God, and Jesus Christ, whom thou hast sent."*

You are saved based on what The Word of God says. You are not saved based on how you feel. I pray that this is settled in your heart.

Even though you are saved, are there areas in your life that you know God is still working on, areas where you know you're not getting it ***all*** right each time you are faced with a particular challenge? Well, let's talk about it.

We exist in three parts: spirit, soul, and body and The

Word of God tells us so! The last part of I Thessalonians 5:23 says, *"... and I pray God your whole spirit and soul and body be preserved blameless unto the coming of our Lord Jesus Christ."* So we exist in three parts: spirit, soul, and body. **Our <u>spirit</u> man has been made righteous** because we accepted Jesus as our Lord and Savior.

Romans 10:10 – *"For with the heart man believeth unto righteousness; and with the mouth confession is made unto salvation."*

Ezekiel 36:26 – *"A new heart also will I give you, and a new spirit will I put within you: and I will take away the stony heart out of your flesh, and I will give you an heart of flesh."*

Physically, we didn't change. There was an old song that said, "My hands are new and my feet are too…" But our hands aren't new and neither are our feet! Our bodies, our flesh as we know it, didn't change. Our <u>*real*</u> heart, our spirit did.

When we invited Jesus Christ into our hearts, our old man (the flesh man) was crucified with Christ and resurrected in newness of life (the spirit man). But even though we were crucified and raised in newness of life, our old man which is flesh, blood, and bone will always try to resurrect, will always try to come back to life because of the sin nature in the flesh. The enemy will try to have us think and act on some of the same things we did before we accepted Jesus Christ as our Lord and Savior. That is why this section is extremely important to our spiritual growth. The Apostle Paul tells us that there is no good thing in our flesh:

Romans 7:18 – *"For I know that in me (that is, in my flesh,) dwelleth no good thing: for to will is present with me; but how to perform that which is good I find not."*

Romans 7:25 – *"I thank God through Jesus Christ our Lord. So then with the mind I myself serve the law of God; but with the flesh the law of sin."*

In order to keep the flesh from serving the law of sin that is in our nature, we have to allow the Holy Spirit, working in us, to <u>**change the way we think**</u>, so that He can work the Will of God out through our flesh!

Remember that **our bodies (our flesh as we know it) didn't change, our <u>real</u> heart, our spirit did.** The Word of God says, in Romans 7:18a that there is nothing good in our flesh.

Romans 7:18a – *"For I know that in me (that is, in my flesh,) dwelleth no good thing:"*

We are still flesh, bone, and blood and because of the way our flesh used to act and react before we accepted Christ, it wants to keep doing what it used to do. Our flesh immediately tries to gain control of the new heart that God gave us. Our flesh tries to resurrect! It does this through trying to get us to think and act on evil thoughts and desires instead of the Word of God! There is a war going on for control of our thought life! Whoever you obey is the one who has gained control.

Romans 6:16 – *"Know ye not, that to whom ye yield yourselves servants to obey, his servants ye are to whom ye obey; whether of sin unto death, or of obedience unto righteousness?"*

Keep in mind that the **"real"** you is a spirit man, who lives in a flesh and blood body, and has a soul (mind). Jesus said in John 3:6, *"That which is born of the flesh is flesh; and that which is born of the Spirit is spirit."* You are a spirit being! You are a man, woman, boy, or girl who is in three dimensions—spirit, soul, and body! That man can be one of three men: a fleshly man, a spiritual man, or a carnal man.

We talked about the unregenerate man. That unregenerate man is a ***fleshly man*** who has never accepted Jesus Christ as Lord and Savior. The ***spiritual man*** is walking in those things that please God. The ***carnal man*** has accepted Jesus Christ as Lord and Savior but is still walking after the things of the world, taking part in activities that don't please God.

There is the ***old man, the fleshly man,*** who we once were, who was lost in sin and whose heart had not been changed. And now there is the ***new man*** who is in Christ whose heart is changed. The <u>***new man (the real you) is spirit***</u>. This bears repeating: The <u>***new man (the real you) is spirit!***</u> The old man is flesh, bone, and blood. The old man wants to keep on satisfying those things that the flesh loved to do and say. The new man, the real you, your spirit man, longs to satisfy God and to do those things that are pleasing in His Sight!

When we accepted Jesus Christ, we were "crucified" with Him and "raised" with Him to eternal life.

Romans 6:6 – *"Knowing this, that our old man is crucified with him, that the **body of sin** might be destroyed, that henceforth we should not serve sin."*

This "body of sin" in the Scripture signifies our flesh. Jesus took our sins upon himself and died in our place so that our "flesh" would be destroyed so that we no longer would serve sin, but serve The Lord.

Romans 6:4 – *"...that like as Christ was raised up from the dead by the glory of the Father, **even so we** also should walk in newness of life."*

Romans 6:11 – *"Likewise **reckon** ye also yourselves to be dead indeed unto sin, but alive unto God through Jesus Christ our Lord."*

Romans 8:10 – *"And if Christ be in you, the body is dead because of sin; but the Spirit is **life** because of righteousness."*

Our flesh "died," but we find that sometimes our flesh tries to resurrect from the dead. Those old fleshly desires want to come back. That's when the battle comes and the resurrected life of Jesus in us will win if we allow Him to. Who will live? Do we allow the Spirit of God in us to reign, or do we allow the flesh to dominate? Whoever you obey is in control. Remember, our flesh died with Christ and resurrected with Him in newness of life!

How we view ourselves determines who will win! As a man or woman, boy or girl thinks in their heart, that's who they really are (Proverbs 23:7)! We have to think what God thinks about us and say what the Word of God says about us!

We talked about the precious promises that are ours in Christ. Everything that pertains to life and godliness is ours **"through the <u>knowledge of him</u> that hath called us to glory and virtue." (2 Peter 1:3)** As we receive the truth of God's Word into our hearts and as we allow those promises to take root and grow in our hearts and minds by The Spirit of God, we are transformed more and more into His image. God's Word commands us to:

Ephesians 4:22-23 *– "That ye put off concerning the former conversation the old man, which is corrupt according to the deceitful lusts; ²³And be **renewed in the spirit of your mind;**" ²⁴And that ye put on the new man, which after God is created in righteousness and true holiness."*

We have been given great and precious promises so that we can be partakers of the Divine Nature of God! What you don't know **_can_** hurt you and hinder your spiritual growth!

2 Peter 1:2-4 – *"²Grace and peace be multiplied unto you **through the knowledge of God**, and of Jesus our Lord, ³According as his divine power hath given unto us all things that pertain unto life and godliness, **through the knowledge of him** that hath called us to glory and virtue: ⁴Whereby are given unto us exceeding great and precious promises: that by these ye might be **partakers of the divine nature**, having escaped the corruption that is in the world through lust."*

True holiness, taking on of the Divine Nature, means that we do not conform to this world. By the Grace of God, we don't act like this world acts.

Romans 12:1-2 – *"I beseech you therefore, brethren, by the mercies of God, that ye present your bodies a living sacrifice, holy, acceptable unto God, which is your reasonable service. ²And be not conformed to this world: but be ye **transformed by the renewing of your mind**, that ye may prove what is that good, and acceptable, and perfect, will of God."*

You might say, "The Word of God tells us to do all these things, but how?" But first, it's important that we know what's going on with our spirit, soul, and body. We are a spirit, we live in a body, and we have a soul.

Of the spirit, soul, and body, ***our spirit man is the most stable***. Of our spirit, soul, and body, ***our body is the least stable of the three***. And then there is the soul of man, where all the battles for control are fought between the soul and spirit for control of our body.

Our spirit has three parts: intuition, communion, and conscience.
1. ***Intuition*** is the intuitive knowledge of God. (I John 2:20; I Corin-thians 2:9-10; John 14:26; John 16:13-15)
2. ***Communion*** is the part that fellowships, has union with God, participates with God, and is one with God. (Psalm 77:6)
3. ***Conscience*** is the part that gives us the ability to tell good and evil: convicts of sin, is sensitive to God, bears witness, lets us know if we have a good conscience, and rejoices. (Hebrews 5:14; Titus 2:11-12; Romans 8:1-2)

Our soul has three parts: intellect, emotions, and will.
1. ***Intellect*** or mind is "the thinker," the reasoner or logical part of our soul. It compares. (Mark 2:6-8; Luke 9:46-47)
2. ***Emotions*** is "the feeler" and tells us what we like or dislike and is the ***most unstable of the soul***. Most decisions are made out of our emotions. (Matthew 26:38-39)
3. ***Will*** is "the decider" and propels us into action. (Matthew 26:38-39)

Our body exists in three parts: flesh, blood, and bone. (Leviticus 17:11a, v14) **Our body** is God's temple (I Corinthians 6:19).

1. ***Flesh*** brings mobility to bone and is the blood container.
2. ***Blood*** (and other fluids related to blood) flows through our flesh, except the skin.
3. ***Bone*** produces blood and gives us shape and structure.

All of these parts of man—spirit, soul, and body, are connected. Our **spirit** man affects the **soul**, and our soul affects our **body**. Let's see how they are connected.

The soul is transformed when the born again spirit man sends The Word to the soul (mind). The soul (mind) by receiving and believing The Word changes the thinking and the mind is transformed. The transformed mind decides to obey The Word and tells the body what to do or to say.

The Spirit sends the Word to the soul; the transformed soul affects the whole body.

It's our decision! God won't force Himself on us. If we choose to obey, it will be evident by what our body does or says. If we choose to disobey, that will be evident as well. If there is no faith in The Word of God and if the spirit of man has not been changed, defeat is inevitable.

The more we hear and obey The Word of God and the more we receive those good thoughts from the Lord and act on them, the stronger we become. Just as food is to our body, so is The Word of God to our souls. If we keep the food we eat in us, we will be nourished by it. But if we don't, we will become weak, undernourished, and can die!

If we keep The Word in us by obeying It and we don't bring It back up, It will strengthen us, become a part of us and as a result, it will be evident to all that Jesus Christ is in our lives. But, if we bring The Word of God back up by not obeying It, that will be evident as well! The saying, "You are what you eat," is as true in the natural as it is in the spiritual. The Word of God is our spiritual food!

Those old ugly thoughts will try to gain control of our souls (minds). But where do those thoughts come from? Those evil thoughts come from the devil, the world, and the flesh. We defeat the devil by using The Word of God. We defeat the world by our faith. We defeat the flesh by the Spirit.

The Word defeats the devil. Jesus used The Word of God in order to defeat satan (Matthew 4 and Luke 4). In every instance where Jesus was tempted, He declared, ***"It is written."*** He was referring to The Word of God!

Our faith overcomes the world. I John 2:16 says, *"For all that is in the world, the lust of the flesh, and the lust of the eyes, and the pride of life, is not of the Father, but is of the world."* I John 5:4 tells us, *"For whatsoever is born of God overcometh the world: and this is the victory that* **overcometh the world, even our faith**.*"*

Submitting to the Spirit of God defeats our flesh. The Word tells us that there is nothing good in our flesh. The works of the flesh are found in Galatians 5:19-21; Ephesians 5:3-8; Colossians 3:5-9. And Romans 8:13b says, *"...if ye **through the <u>Spirit</u> do mortify the deeds of the body**, ye shall live."* The word "mortify" means put to death. The Word of God tells us to submit to God, resist the devil and that the devil will flee from us!

James 4:7 – *"Submit yourselves therefore to God. Resist the devil, and he will flee from you."*

Romans 8:13 – *"For if ye live after the flesh, ye shall die: but if ye through the Spirit do mortify the deeds of the body, ye shall live."*

By the Spirit of God, obey the Word. If there is no faith in the Word sent to the soul, we live in defeat and the soul (mind) is never renewed. Faith in the Word comes by hearing The Word of God over and over and over again!

Romans 10:17 – *"So then faith cometh by hearing, and hearing by the word of God."*

God's Will for us is that we would follow after holiness, that we look and act like Christ, that we allow His Word to be planted in our hearts and minds and take root there and grow, and that we would allow Him to live through us. God's Will for us is sanctification (clean and set apart for God's use). He wants to present us to Himself a glorious Church not having a spot or wrinkle or anything like a spot or wrinkle. He wants us to show the world that we are partakers of His Divine Nature that He might be glorified. (2 Peter 1:4).

Hebrews 12:14 – *"Follow peace with all men, **and holiness**, without which no man shall see the Lord:"*

I Thessalonians 4:3 – *"For this is the will of God, even your **sanctification…**"*

I Thessalonians 5:23 – *"And the very God of peace **sanctify you wholly**; and I pray God your whole spirit and soul and body be preserved blameless unto the coming of our Lord Jesus Christ."*

Ephesians 5:25-27 – *"^{25}Husbands, love your wives, even as Christ also loved the church, and gave himself for it, ^{26}That he might **sanctify and cleanse it with the washing of water by the word**, ^{27}That he might present it to himself a glorious church, not having spot, or wrinkle, or any such thing; but that it should be **holy and without blemish**.*

John 17:17 – *"**Sanctify them through thy truth: thy word is truth**."*

2 Peter 1:3 – *"According as his divine power hath given unto us all things that pertain unto life and godliness, **through the knowledge of him** that hath called us to glory and virtue:"*

2 Peter 1:4 *– "Whereby are given unto us exceeding great and precious promises: that by these ye might be **partakers of the divine nature**, having escaped the corruption that is in the world through lust."*

Jesus is The Word and Jesus <u>*will*</u> clean us up. God wants us to hide His Word in our hearts, He wants us to let the Word of God dwell in us richly (Colossians 3:16). As we allow The Word of God to abide in us, meditate on It and do It; as we allow Christ to live through us, we ***grow*** in grace and in the knowledge of our Lord and Savior Jesus Christ (2 Peter 3:18). Psalm 91 has so many promises in it that are a result of our abiding in Him. Jesus said…

John 15:5 *– "I am the vine, ye are the branches: He that abideth in me, and I in him the same bringeth forth much fruit for <u>**without me ye can do nothing**</u>."*

God knew that we could not do His Word in our own strength. That's why Jesus came, was crucified, rose from the dead, and the Holy Ghost was sent to give us power to live a godly life. All we need to do is trust God to live through us as we present our bodies to Him. Have we "missed it" sometimes, done things contrary to the Will of God? Yes! Each one of us who has ever walked this Christian life has "missed it" at one time or other. But God, in His Mercy, has given us a promise and has provided for us *if* we do sin:

I John 2:1-2 *(NIV) – "[1]My dear children, I write this to you so that you will not sin. But **if** anybody does sin, we have one who speaks to the Father in our defense—Jesus Christ, the Righteous One. [2]He is the atoning sacrifice for our sins, and not only for ours but also for the sins of the whole world."*

I John 1:9 *(NIV) – "If we confess our sins, He is faithful and righteous to forgive us our sins and to cleanse us from all unrighteousness."*

Romans 8:1 *– "There is therefore now no condemnation to them which are in Christ Jesus, who walk not after the flesh, but after the Spirit."*

2 Corinthians 12:9a *– "And he said unto me, My grace is sufficient for thee: for my strength is made perfect in weakness…."*

Jesus has experienced everything we experience yet He was without sin. In Hebrews 4:15 it says, *"For we have not an high priest which cannot be touched with the feeling of our infirmities; but was in all points tempted like as we are, yet without sin."* Our Father God never condemns us, but He will correct us and His Mercy and Grace are there to help us in our time of need. You don't have to beg God. He is our Father and His love for us is unconditional. He wants us to come boldly to Him, not arrogantly, but humbly and in reverence to obtain the grace we need.

Hebrews 4:16 – *"Let us therefore come boldly unto the throne of grace, that we may obtain mercy, and find grace to help in time of need."*

If we could live a sin-free life in our own strength, there would have been no need for Jesus to have come on earth. But He came to set us free from the power of sin and death!

Our Father God doesn't want us to be afraid to come to Him when we need help. He doesn't want us to hide from Him as Adam did when he sinned. God knows exactly what we are doing and what we are going through anyway and He loves us just the same.

If you have sinned, just believe that God loves you unconditionally and receive the forgiveness that has already been provided. God's grace will give you the strength you need to stand, and when you have done all you can do to stand, we are told to keep on standing! Not in our own strength, but the strength of The Lord! (Ephesians 6:10-18)

Remember, you have been forgiven of all sins; past, present, and future sins. They are forgotten by God and forever nailed to the cross of Jesus. When you go before Him trying to remind Him of sins, He doesn't remember them because He sees the shed Blood of Jesus covering you. He has already forgiven you!

Jesus took our sins upon Himself and clothed us in His righteousness—that's what God sees. He sees us righteous; as though we had never sinned! (I John 1:9; I John 2:1-2; Romans 8:1-2; Romans 12:1-2; Psalm 103:12; Ephesians 4:24; Romans 5:21; Romans 5:17-18; Ephesians 2:8-9; Colossians 2:14).

Chapter 3
"Preparing for Battle"

A part of growing up spiritually is our preparation for fighting an effectual warfare against the enemy! Our Father wants us to subdue and to take dominion! We are more than conquerors through Him Who loves us and has given His Life for us!

Know Who You Are

We *must* know whose we are and who we are in Christ! Know that when you accepted Jesus Christ as your Lord and Savior that you were crucified with Him and raised together with Him in newness of life. Know that you have been given power and authority to defeat the enemy. Know that you have been delivered from the power of sin and death! Know that you have been forgiven of all sins; past, present, and future sins! Should we continue in sin just because we know that we are forgiven? No!!! **Romans 6:1-2** – *"¹What shall we say then? Shall we continue in sin, that grace may abound? ²God forbid. How shall we, that are dead to sin, live any longer therein?*

God does not want us to use the liberty that we were given to sin. Although God has forgiven you and will forgive, His grace is not to be used as an excuse to sin or to be used as a so-called "get out of jail free card."

Galatians 5:13 – *"For, brethren, ye have been called unto liberty; only use not liberty for an occasion to the flesh, but **by love serve** one another."*

I John 2:1 – *"My little children, these things write I unto you, that ye sin not. And **if** any man sin, we have an advocate with the Father, Jesus Christ the righteous:*

"If" in I John 2:1 is conditional. "If" means that we don't have to sin, but "if" we do, provision has been made for us. But our Father does not expect us to practice sin. Because He loves us, if we do sin, our Father will forgive.

Romans 5:20b-21 – *"²⁰ᵇ…But where sin abounded, grace did much more abound: ²¹That as sin hath reigned unto death, even so might grace reign through righteousness unto eternal life by Jesus Christ our Lord."*

The love of God for us, our love for Him, and our love for people should cause us to want to allow Jesus to live through us  and to allow His Grace to keep us from sinning! And He will live through us if we let Him. He will not force Himself on us, but He will help us live a victorious life. He is our Helper, our Standby, our Keeper, our Very Present Help in times of trouble, He's our Comforter. Just ask Him to help you and He will! (Hebrews 13:6; Psalm 121:5; Psalm 46:1; John 14:26)

Many people are defeated in their Christian walk with God because they simply do not prepare themselves for battle. In the military as well as in the sports arena, a battle plan is laid out. The enemy in the field, and the challenging team on the turf have been studied. If studying the opposition in the natural is true, how much more true is it in the spiritual! God does not want us to be ignorant or unknowledgeable of the devil's devices, his plots, plans, and schemes.

But, keep in mind that our battle is not against other humans. Our fight is against the devil! A spiritual enemy! The devil will use humans many times and those humans may not even be aware that they are being used by the devil. That's all the more reason why we need to keep in mind who the real enemy is! We are fighting a spiritual battle against a spiritual devil!

Ephesians 6:12 – *"For we wrestle not against flesh and blood, but against principalities [princes over certain territories], against* *powers, against the rulers of the darkness of this world, against spiritual wickedness in high places."*

2 Corinthians 10:3-6 *– "³For though we walk in the flesh, we do not war after the flesh; ⁴(For the weapons of our warfare are not carnal, but mighty through God to the pulling down of strong holds;)* **⁵Casting down imaginations, and every high thing that exalteth itself against the <u>knowledge of God</u>,** *and bringing into captivity every thought to the obedience of Christ; ⁶And having in a readiness to revenge all disobedience, when your obedience is fulfilled."*

And keep in mind that everything you need in order to be victorious in this life was given to you when you accepted Jesus Christ as your Lord and Savior. When Jesus was crucified, He said, "It is finished!" It's done! Your job is to cast down those evil thoughts that come and replace them with Godly thoughts, with The Word of God! You must use the authority you have been given to subdue the flesh by the spirit and dominate!

<u>Temptation and Sin</u>

<u>Temptation is not sin</u>. Jesus was tempted yet without sin. ***Temptation*** is "***<u>the devil's attempt</u>*** to get the believer to disobey God" (Robbins 25). Temptation will come from one of three places: **1)** the world around you, **2)** your own flesh, or **3)** the devil. A Minister once said, "Birds can fly over your head, but you don't have to let them build a nest there!" Just because the temptation comes does not mean that you have to submit to it! The devil will have you think that you are the only one going through what you are going through, that you are in this battle all by yourself and that there is no way out! He is a liar and the father of lies!

I Corinthians 10:13 – *"There hath no temptation taken you **but such as is common to man**: but God is faithful, who will not suffer you to be tempted above that ye are able; but will with the temptation also make a way to escape, that ye may be able to bear it."*

Note that the Scripture says, "but such as is common to man" which means that whatever temptation you might face, every man, woman, boy, and girl has faced or will face it at some time in their life. Not only that, God will not allow you to be tempted with anything that will destroy you but will always make a way of escape so that you will be victorious. It's up to us to take the way of escape that He has already provided. I heard a Minister once say, "Nothing touches our lives that is not first Father filtered." Meaning that God already knows that by His Grace, we can handle whatever comes our way. There is nothing too hard or impossible for God, and we can do all things through Christ Who strengthens us (Luke 1:37; Philippians 4:13)!

You don't have to "entertain" the thoughts if they come. You don't have to dwell on them, tossing them around in your mind thinking about them—you can submit to God's Word, ***resist*** the devil and he ***will flee!*** You can also ***avoid*** those places, persons, and things that ***you know*** will cause you to sin (television shows, movies, music, etc.). What someone else may be able to do and not sin, you may not be able to do. Know yourself! "Avoid the temptation where possible and resist temptation when avoiding it is not possible…" (Robbins 25, paraphrased).

I Corinthians 15:33 (Amplified) – *"Do not be deceived: 'Bad company corrupts good morals'."*

"Sin is knowing the will of God for your life and choosing to do otherwise." (Robbins 9) ***Sin is knowing God's Will and choosing not to obey God, period!*** But you don't have to sin! You can submit to The Spirit of God in you, speak out The Word of God. I John 4:4 tells us that greater is He that is in us than he that is in the world! Resist the devil and he will flee! That's a promise to us!

James 4:7 – *"Submit yourselves therefore to God. Resist the devil, and he will flee from you."*

It may hurt to submit, but crucifying the flesh always does. The Word of God tells us that we are to ***arm ourselves, our minds*** for suffering. The suffering comes from resisting, denying, and crucifying our flesh!

I Peter 4:1 – *"Forasmuch then as Christ hath suffered for us in the flesh, arm yourselves likewise with the same mind: **for he that hath suffered in the flesh hath ceased from sin:**"*

Since we know that the mind is where all our battles are won or lost, wisdom tells us that we will need to arm our minds for battle. We need to arm ourselves with The Word of God!

Rest assured that if you will submit to The Word God and resist the devil, you will be victorious in every area of your life! God is able to deliver you out of anything that may have you bound and it is by The Power of The Holy Spirit! Once delivered, you can stay delivered, but it doesn't mean that the enemy will not try to get back into your life. Jesus was without sin. After tempting Jesus, the devil only left Jesus for a season, so you know the devil will try again to tempt us (Luke 4:13)! But we can be victorious in every spiritual battle we fight! The more we submit to God, the stronger we get!

The devil can't make you sin and he has no new tricks to use in order to try to get us to sin. He can only tempt us with whatever he has available to him. He can only tempt us with what we are familiar with, those things that have already been crucified in our flesh by our baptism into the body of Jesus when He died. He only uses those things that we have already experienced or those things that he has used on others. We just have to remember and confess that we are "dead" to sin and alive unto Jesus Christ! Don't let your flesh resurrect! Submit to God and resist the devil! **Romans 6:3-4, 6** – *"[3]Know ye not, that so many of us as were baptized into Jesus Christ were baptized into his death? [4]Therefore we are buried with him by baptism into death: that like as Christ was raised up from the dead by the glory of the Father, even so we* *also should walk in newness of life….*⁶*Knowing this, that our old man is crucified with him, that the body of sin might be destroyed, that henceforth we should not serve sin."*

Galatians 2:20 – *"I am crucified with Christ: nevertheless I live; yet not I, but Christ liveth in me: and the life which I now live in the flesh* **I live by the faith of the Son of God**, *who loved me, and gave himself for me."*

James 1:13-15 – *"Let no man say when he is tempted, I am tempted of God: for God cannot be tempted with evil, neither tempteth he any man:* ¹⁴***But every man is tempted, when he is drawn away of his own lust, and enticed.*** ¹⁵*Then when lust hath conceived, it bringeth forth sin: and sin, when it is finished, bringeth forth death."*

    We are still preparing for the battle, and remember, the battle takes place in our minds. We are told to gird up the loins of our minds and to be sober, to be vigilant, to prepare for action, to put on the **_helmet_** of salvation (I Peter 1:13a; I Peter 5:8; Ephesians 6:17). That helmet covers our mind (soul). Resist those ungodly thoughts and replace them with God's Word! Remind the devil that he is a defeated foe! Know that Jesus finished the work! It's done!

Chapter 4
"Guarding Your Mind (Soul)!"

The mind and soul are used interchangeably, and the enemy is strategic in attacking it. Our mind is where all the battles are won or lost! Knowing how the enemy attacks is key to being able to defeat him.

<u>**How The Enemy Attacks Our Soul**</u>

The first stage, <u>the emotions</u>. Because there is no good "thing" in our flesh, whatever ***<u>has not</u>*** been submitted to God is fair game. Whenever that "thing" presents itself, if you don't immediately submit to The Word of God and resist it, what happens is that the enemy will try to draw you away from obeying

God by talking to your mind and playing with your thoughts and ***your emotions.***

He'll try to use things like, "it looks good, felt good, tasted good, sounds good, etc." You may not even know that it's in your flesh until it presents itself *or* you may have believed that it was dead! And it is dead, but your flesh is trying to resurrect and your emotions are trying to help bring it back to life! Ask yourself, "What triggered it?" What caused your flesh to try to resurrect? Avoid the trigger!

You have to **speak to your flesh** and remind your flesh that it is **DEAD**! Remember, the emotions is a part of your soul or mind and is the *"feeler."* It remembers how things or people used to make you feel. ***But you have to know that you are dead to "that thing" and that your life is hid with Christ in God! And tell the devil so! We walk by faith not by our senses!***

Colossians 3:3 – *"For ye are **dead**, and your life is hid with Christ in God."*

Galatians 2:20 – *"I am crucified with Christ: nevertheless I live; yet not I, but Christ liveth in me: and the life which I now live in the flesh I live **by the faith of the Son of God**, who loved me, and gave himself for me."*

This is where 2 Corinthians 10:5 comes into play. The emotions get attacked by the "trigger." Your ***spirit man*** gets involved and you get a little "check" or warning from the inside saying, "don't do that." That's when you ***"Cast down every imagination and high thing that exalts itself above the knowledge of God, and bring into captivity every thought to the obedience of Christ!"*** You do this by asking for the help of The Holy Spirit, submitting to The Word of God in you, speaking that Word to the "thing," and let Jesus Christ in you live through you.

Know yourself! Don't wait until the devil attacks! Be ready for him! Find Scriptures in your Bible for what you are believing for and speak that Word out loud! The Spirit of God is our Helper! You are armed with The Word of God! Speak it out over and over again if you have to, resist the devil and rest in and trust Jesus to do the work through you. He will!

It is so much easier to resist the thought when it first presents itself than to give in and have to go through the same thing over and over again until you pass the test. Good point to remember—***it's only a test***! But that test will become harder and harder the more you give in to the temptation! But God's Mercy still stands true! He will provide the strength you need to pass every test!

James 1:14-15 *– "But every man is tempted, when he is drawn away of his own lust, and enticed.* ^(15)*Then when lust hath conceived; it bringeth forth sin: and sin, when it is finished, bringeth forth **death**."*

The second stage, <u>the intellect</u>. If you begin to entertain "that thing," whatever it might be, what will happen is that you start to evaluate it, reason with it—that's **your intellect**, the **"*thinker,*"** coming into play. You begin to reason with it saying to yourself things like, "I remember how that felt, how it tasted, how it sounded, etc." Your **spirit man** gets involved again and you get another little "check" or warning from the inside saying, "You shouldn't think that, you shouldn't say that, you shouldn't go there, you shouldn't do that, etc." Then the enemy says, "Oh, just a little won't hurt." The intellect/reasoner/thinker says, "Maybe it won't, just a little." "I won't go all the way, I'm strong enough to stop before I go too far," "I got this result the last time I did it, I'll do it again," "God will forgive you." ***<u>You're now in denial!</u>*** And the enemy has enticed you, he's drawn you into the sin! You start thinking on it more and more! ***<u>The temptation is not the sin, yielding to it is! Entertaining it in your mind is!</u>*** You have been arguing with your spirit man who is trying to stop you!

During this stage, you have an opportunity to again cast the thought down and ask for forgiveness before you are led to carry the temptation out in your body. If you think on anything long enough, you will do it! You will eventually carry it out! *As a man thinketh in his heart so is he! (Proverbs 23:7)* ***<u>Cast the thought down immediately!</u>***

The third stage—<u>the will</u>. The "will" decides. During the first and second stage, the will has been ***"deciding"*** as to whether to do or not to do. It now decides whether to yield to the temptation and give in, to obey or to disobey. The will decides whether to do what the spirit man is saying or to do what the flesh man is saying. The will has the final say as to whether to obey or to disobey the Spirit of God. If you decide in your mind to do "the thing," lust has conceived and if pursued, brings forth evident sin, and when the devil is finished, that sin that you have been tempted with and gone through with brings forth death and this doesn't necessarily mean natural death. You might find yourself not being able to pray, read The Word, witness, worship, etc. like you used to.

James 1:14-15 – *"But every man is tempted, when he is drawn away of his own lust, and enticed. ^{15}Then when lust hath conceived, it bringeth forth sin: and sin, when it is finished, bringeth forth death."*

But it's not over yet because the next step is that after the devil has tempted you and you have yielded to the temptation and obeyed his lies, he now tries to condemn you. But even so, you can be forgiven. Are you walking after the Spirit of God? Do you want to live a holy life before God?

Romans 8:1 – *"There is therefore now no condemnation to them which are in Christ Jesus, who walk not after the flesh, but after the Spirit."*

Your soul is where the battles are fought and your will determines whether to obey or to disobey God. Remember, any thoughts that are contrary to the Will of God must be cast down immediately.

Chapter 5
"Defeating the Enemy"

The most important Person some people overlook when going into battle against the forces of darkness is The Person of The Holy Ghost (Spirit)! Jesus commands us to be filled with The Spirit. If Jesus didn't think it was necessary, He would never have given the command. The Holy Spirit gives us the ability to pray the perfect will of God down into every situation we face. When we don't know what to pray or how to pray, the Spirit of God helps us:

Romans 8:26-27 *(NIV) – "[26]In the same way, the Spirit helps us in our weakness. We do not know what we ought to pray for, but the Spirit himself intercedes for us with groans that words cannot express. [27]And he who searches our hearts knows the mind of the*

Spirit, because the Spirit intercedes for the saints in accordance with God's will."

Jude 20-21 – *"[20]But ye, beloved, building up yourselves on your most holy faith, praying in the Holy Ghost, [21]Keep yourselves in the love of God, looking for the mercy of our Lord Jesus Christ unto eternal life."*

<u>The Holy Spirit gives us power to witness, walk, work, war, and worship.</u> (Acts 1:8; Acts 4:31; Acts 2:11; I Corinthians 14:15; Romans 18:26-27; Ephesians 6:18) We are more than conquerors over sin and death because of the Shed Blood of Jesus and His Resurrection Power!

Knowing who we are in Christ and what He has done for us and on our behalf will give us to be victorious in battle against the enemy in our flesh as well as our spiritual enemies. Jesus died, resurrected from the dead, and gave us authority to trample on serpents and scorpions and over all the power of the enemy. He promised us that nothing, by any means, would harm us! Jesus is the Holiness of God, extended to us! His Righteousness is a gift by grace given to us by God (Ephesians 2:8-9; Romans 5:17). Because of the shed Blood of Jesus, we are now clothed in His Righteousness and we are forgiven of all sin! We were saved by grace through faith, and God's grace will keep us free from sin.

Not In Our Own Strength!

God wants us to grow in grace and in the knowledge of Him, but He does not want us to try to do it in our own strength. We have learned how the devil will try to attack us in our thought life and how we can defeat him. But we cannot defeat him in our own strength. Our weapons are not fleshly weapons. They are spiritual weapons to be used against a spiritual enemy.

God wants us, commands us to be holy as He is Holy and He would never ask us to do something that we were not able to do. That's why He has given us His Holy Spirit and we can only do it with His help, our Helper, The Holy Spirit! Speak the Word of God which is Spirit! Pray in tongues and pray with your understanding!

When you try to live a holy life and try to fight an effectual warfare against the enemy in your own strength, it then becomes self-righteousness and we fail time and time again! God wants us to trust and rely on Him to do the work through us as we yield our members as servants to obey Him! He wants us sensitive to the leading and to the direction of His Spirit!

Romans 12:1-2 – *"I beseech you therefore, brethren, by the mercies of God, that ye present your bodies a **living** sacrifice, holy, acceptable unto God, which is your reasonable service. ²And be not conformed to this world: but be ye **transformed by the**

renewing of your mind, *that ye may prove what is that good, and acceptable, and perfect, will of God."*

Romans 8:14 – *"For as many as are led by the Spirit of God, they are the sons of God."*

God wants us righteousness conscious not sin conscious. The work of salvation has been accomplished in our lives by the death, burial, and resurrection of Jesus Christ. Sin consciousness keeps us focused on sin and its hold over us. Sin is the product of Adam's transgression and righteousness is the result of Jesus Christ's obedience—Christ is in us the hope of glory! God has removed sin from us, as far as the east is from the west (Psalm 103:12) and He remembers it no more and He has clothed us in His righteousness. We are not "sinners saved by grace," but we are now saints of the Most High God! We are priests and kings! We are made in the image and likeness of God and can do all things through Christ Who strengthens us!

2 Peter 3:18a – *"But grow in grace, and **in the knowledge** of our Lord and Saviour Jesus Christ…"*

2 Corinthians 5:21 – *"For he hath made him to be sin for us, who knew no sin; that we might be made the righteousness of God in him."*

Philippians 3:9 – *"And be found in him, not having mine own righteousness, which is of the law, but that which is through **the faith of Christ,** the righteousness which is of God by faith:"*

Romans 5:19 – *"For as by one man's disobedience many were made sinners, so by the obedience of one shall many be made righteous."*

Hebrews 4:9 – *There remaineth therefore a rest to the people of God.*

God does not want us to *try* to live a holy life, that's self-righteousness. It failed for Israel. That's why Jesus came into this world. Jesus came to take away our sins once and for all time; not just cover them, but completely remove them. If we could live a Godly life in our own strength, then Jesus would never have had to come. But He did. Jesus came into our hearts and wants to live through us and He will if we allow Him to! Not only that, but The Holy Ghost was sent back to help us live a holy life before God. Ephesians 2:8-9; 2 Corinthians 5:21; I Corinthians 1:30; Romans 3:20-22; 2 Peter 3:18; Philippians 3:9. God's Grace helps us live a Godly life. But this Grace should never be used as an excuse or crutch to keep on sinning. ***<u>The Holy Spirit of God is our Helper to keep us from sinning.</u>***

More Ammunition for the Battle

Jesus spoke to the devil; so must we. We have to ***say what God's Word says***. God's Word tells us that faith comes by hearing and hearing by The Word of God. When we speak The Word out loud, we hear it!

Find Scriptures in the Word to pray to God. He tells us to bring Him in remembrance of It, to state your case to Him. He says that He watches over His Word to perform it in our lives. He also tells us that if we ask anything according to ***His Will***, He hears us and because we know that He hears us, we know that we have what we have desired. (Isaiah 43:26; Jeremiah 1:12; I John 5:14-15)

Just as we have a "Last Will and Testament" in the natural, God's Word is His Will to and for us! We have the Old and New Testaments. If you don't open God's Word and read It you will not know what has been given to you or what you are entitled to! ***God's "Will" is His Word!***

The Word of God tells us in Philippians 4:8 that we should ***think on things that are true, honest, just, pure, lovely, of good report, virtuous, praiseworthy things.*** If the thoughts that come are not these thoughts, cast them down! If they are not righteousness, peace, and joy in The Holy Ghost, cast them down! Some of the ways we can defeat the devil:

- Know who you are in Christ – Romans 8:37; 2 Corinthians 5:21
- Know God loves you unconditionally – John 3:16; Romans 5:8
- We defeat the devil by using the Word of God – Matthew 4:4, 7, 10; James 4:7
- We defeat the world by our faith – I John 5:4
- We defeat the flesh through The Spirit of God – Romans 8:13

- Cast down every imagination and high thing that exalts itself against the knowledge of God – 2 Corinthians 10:4-5
- Replace evil thoughts with God's Word – find the Scriptures in the Word of God that deal with the challenges you have and meditate on that Word. Speak it out.
- Present your body to God – Romans 12:1-2; 2 Corinthians 5:21

- God gives more grace; submit to God's Word; resist the devil – James 4:6-7
- Walk in the Spirit – Galatians 5:16; Romans 8:1, 13-14
- He will keep whatever you ask Him to keep – 2 Timothy 1:12
- The Fruit of the Spirit will be evident – Galatians 5:22-23
- Your life will prove the Will of God – Romans 12:2

God inhabits the praises of His people—so **sing, praise, and worship Him!** In **Ephesians 6:10-18** we are told to put on the whole armor of God so that we will be able to stand against the wiles of the devil and we are told what that armor is.

First of all we are told:
- To be strong in the Lord.
- To put the armor on. We are never to take it off!
- That we are wrestling against the unseen forces of darkness.
- To take the armor up.
- To take it up so that we will be able to withstand in the evil days.
- When we have done all, to **stand! Stand!**

Here's your armor:
- Your loins girt about with **truth**.
- The breastplate of **righteousness**.
- Your feet are shod with the preparation of the gospel of **peace**.
- The shield of **faith** to quench all the fiery darts of the wicked.
- The helmet of **salvation**.
- The sword of the Spirit which is **The Word of God**.
- **Praying always** with all prayer and supplication in the Spirit. Acknowledge God in all your ways, asking Him about **every** decision you make whether large or small.
- Don't just be concerned about yourself, but **watch and pray for all the saints**.

Notice that all of the armor is spiritual armor. There is no armor for our back. We are not designed by our Father for retreat! We are designed to advance and to win! Be renewed in the spirit of your mind and let the Holy Spirit live through you!

Chapter 6
"The Seed"
"Hindrances vs. Freedom to Grow"

Mark 4:14 *– "The sower soweth the word. ^{15}And these are they <u>by the way side</u>, where the word is sown; but when they have heard, Satan cometh immediately, and taketh away the word that was sown in their* 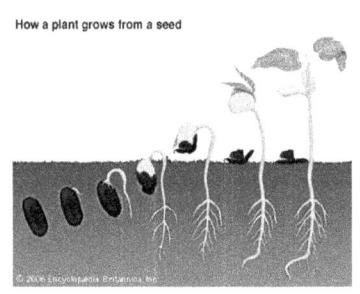 *hearts. ^{16}And these are they likewise which are <u>sown on stony ground</u>; who, when they have heard the word, immediately receive it with gladness; ^{17}And have no root in themselves, and so endure but for a time: afterward, when affliction or persecution ariseth for the word's sake, immediately they are offended. ^{18}And these are* *they which are <u>sown among thorns</u>; such as hear the word, ⁱ⁹And the cares of this world, and the deceitfulness of riches, and the lusts of other things entering in, choke the word, and it becometh unfruitful. ²⁰And these are they which are <u>sown on good ground</u>; such as hear the word, and receive it, and bring forth fruit, some thirtyfold, some sixty, and some an hundred."*

Notice that The Word of God is sown, but that it falls on four types of ears (Mark 4:21-22):

(1) The Word was devoured. It fell on the ears of those who satan immediately stole It from! They let satan steal The Word out of their hearts!

(2) The Word on stony ground—no root. The Word fell on the ears of those who were glad to hear It, tried to do The Word in their own strength but when trying times and persecution came as a result of them speaking or doing the Word they became offended.

(3) The Word among thorns—it's choked. Then there were those who heard The Word, but the cares of the world, deceitfulness of riches and the lust of other things entering into their hearts occupied "the throne" that only God should sit on and those things choked the Word—they lost their testimony!

(4) The Word on good ground. The Word also fell on good ground, those who heard The Word, received The Word and brought forth fruit! They took what they had heard, understood

The Word, and allowed the Holy Spirit to do the work through them, "ran with It," and produced fruit! Fruit, more fruit, and much fruit!

Jesus used many parables which are natural, real-life stories to illustrate a spiritual principle. Mark 4:21-22 is very significant because it follows immediately behind this parable. There is something there that Jesus wants us to see:

Mark 4:21-22 – *"²¹Is a candle bought to be put under a bushel, or under a bed? And not to be set on a candlestick? ²²For there is nothing hid, which shall not be manifested; neither was anything kept secret, but that it should come abroad. ²³If any man have ears to hear, let him hear."*

Our Father God doesn't just want us to hear His Word, let the devil steal it out of our hearts, try to self-righteously do the Word in our own strength, or let anything in this world choke His Word out of us! He expects us to be victorious using every weapon of our warfare He has provided for us! He expects us to be powerful witnesses in a dying, sin-darkened world! **He wants our lights to shine**, not hidden or silenced by the enemy! **He wants us productive**—to allow Him to reproduce through us! We were bought with the price of His Own Blood and He expects our witness to be shared, unhindered by the forces of darkness! The eyes of The Lord are in every place beholding the evil and the good (Proverbs 15:3)! Wherever there is darkness, the Light of the Gospel will dispel it!

When a man and woman come together, "become one," as husband and wife, children are produced out of that union. God wants spiritual children! The Apostle Paul says in:

Ephesians 5:31-32 *"^{31}For this cause shall a man leave his father and mother, and shall be joined unto his wife, and they two shall be one flesh. ^{32}***This is a great mystery: but I speak concerning Christ and the church.***"*

As it is in the natural, so it is in the spiritual. Children are conceived and born as a result of the union between the fertile husband and the fertile wife! Well, God wants spiritual children! As we have learned, if we do not keep The Word of God in our hearts and in our minds and allow The Word to work in our lives, we become ineffective as witnesses—infertile and unproductive! God's Word tells us to be doers of The Word and not just hearers only. We have to cooperate with The Holy Spirit! Remember, He's not going to force us to read His Word and study It, to pray, to worship, to speak His Word into situations we are faced with in life. He is not going to make us stop telling or listening to unsavory jokes, watch ungodly movies, gossip, or listen to music that does not line up with His Word. We have to be willing to submit our will to His in order to grow.

As it is in the natural, so it is in the spiritual. God, plus water, plus sunlight, plus patience causes plants to grow, mature, and reproduce. With a human being, God, The Word, and patience, helps the child to develop and grow, mature, and reproduce. So

Jesus the Son of God, The Word made Flesh, The Bread of Life, The Holy Ghost, The Living Water, gives Life to everything He touches including our spirit man and causes it to reproduce after its own kind! The more that Living Water touches our lives and we absorb Him, we "eat" the Word keeping It in our hearts, letting It transform us, the more we will grow by leaps and bounds and find that we will begin to look and act just like Christ and others will be saved as a result!

John 6:35 *– "And Jesus said unto them, I am the bread of life: he that cometh to me shall never hunger; and he that believeth on me shall never thirst."*

As we are washed with water by The Word of God, presenting our bodies as living sacrifices, crucified flesh yet alive in Jesus Christ, as we are renewed in the spirit of our minds, and as we allow God's Word to work in our lives, our faith will increase, we will grow! (Ephesians 5:26-27; Romans 12: 1; John 4:13)

In ***John 12:24-25 Jesus said:*** *"²⁴Except a corn of wheat fall into the ground and die, it abideth alone: but if it die, it bringeth forth much fruit. ²⁵He that loveth his life shall lose it; and he that hateth his life in this world shall keep it unto life eternal."*

That seed died in order for another stalk to grow and produce more wheat. We are told to present our bodies as living sacrifices, holy and acceptable unto God which is our reasonable service. Our bodies don't want to experience the pain of crucifixion, the dying (or denying) of our flesh. It still wants to do the things it used to do. The flesh is selfish! Jesus said:

Matthew 16:24 – *"Then said Jesus unto his disciples, If any man will come after me, let him deny himself, and **take up his cross**, and follow me."*

And **Galatians 2:20** – *"**I am crucified with Christ**: nevertheless I live; yet not I, but Christ liveth in me: and the life which I now live in the flesh I live by the faith of the Son of God, who loved me, and gave himself for me."*

We are dead to sin, but alive unto God through Jesus Christ! We must keep our flesh crucified, hidden in Christ! We want to be so submitted to God and in union with His Word, His Son Jesus, that **we will be productive, producing good fruit** so that God will be glorified. God wants more children in His family! He wants the same thing now that He wanted for Adam and Eve. He wants <u>us</u> to be fruitful and multiply, replenish the earth, and subdue it and dominate it! Not just in a natural sense, but also in a spiritual sense!

We cannot birth spiritual children of God if we are not submitted to Him, just as the wife is submitted to her husband! As we hear God's Word and submit to It, resisting the devil whenever he tries to tempt us, trusting The Holy Spirit working through us to help keep our flesh dead, we grow, we are patient during the process, and we mature! We are fertile! We reproduce!

But, on the other hand, if we ***only hear*** and do not allow the Holy Spirit to work God's Word out in and through us, we deceive ourselves.

James 1:22 – "*²²But **be ye doers of the word**, and not hearers only, **deceiving** your own selves.*"

...and DO

The Word also says in ***2 Timothy 3:13***, "*But evil men and seducers shall wax worse and worse, **deceiving,** and being deceived.*" We do not want to deceive our own selves and we do not want to be deceived. We do not want to be found doing anything that would hinder our witness!

You have freedom to grow! You are "fertile ground!" You have been given freedom from ***all*** sin as a result of your having accepted Jesus Christ as your Lord and Savior! Only don't use it as an excuse to sin! Use God's Grace, His unmerited favor, to help keep you from sinning! Grow in grace and in the knowledge of our Lord and Savior Jesus Christ! You are more than a conqueror!

John 8:36 – "*If the Son therefore shall make you free, ye shall be free indeed.*"

*Hindrances to Growth**

- Lack of exposure to the five-fold Ministry Gifts – ***Ephesians 4:11***
- Not being fed the sincere "milk of The Word" – ***I Peter 2:2***
- Not desiring The Word and acting on It – ***Matthew 5:6; James 1:22***
- Not being a doer of the word (listen, hear, obey) – ***James 1:22***
- Having a prideful, haughty spirit – ***I Peter 5:5***
- False teaching and wrong leadership – ***2 Peter 2:1; Matthew 15:14***
- Being carnal minded – ***Romans 8:6***
- Unforgiveness and bitterness – ***Mark 11:25-26; Hebrews 12:14-15***
- Being double-minded – ***James 1:8***
- Hardened heart, disobedient to The Word (saying "No" to God) – ***Hebrews 4:7***
- Not accepting correction or counsel – ***Proverbs 15:10; 2 Timothy 3:16-17***
- Fellowship with those who do not desire to grow – ***Ephesians 5:11; Amos 3:3***
- Becoming content where you are/not wanting to grow anymore – ***2 Peter 3:18***
- Lacking a loving environment (you can overcome it) – ***John 13:34; I John 4:11***

---

*Whetstone, pp. 14-22 paraphrased.

Immature Christian	vs.	**The Mature Christian****
Studies the Word only while being taught		*Studies the Word on his own*
Expresses anxiety continually		*Has the peace of God in his heart*
Imitates others (dress, behavior, etc.)		*Imitates Christ; has his own style*
Thinks he knows it all		*Acknowledges God for direction*
Insists on his own way		*Recognizes Jesus is The Way*
Avoids responsibility		*Takes charge, is responsible*
Tires easily when excitement lessens		*Receives from any Vessel*
Only thinks of himself		*Thinks of others continually*
Cries a lot, needs attention, gossips		*Does not complain or gossip*
Affected by cliques and peer groups		*Sets the standard that others desire*
Takes everything as a personal offense		*Does not take things personally*
Always looking for "a word"/direction		*Knows how to seek God's Will*
Walks after "the water is parted"		*Parts water, steps in, others follow*
Puts others down to lift himself up		*Lifts others up*
Requires constant direction		*Led by The Spirit of God*
They make messes		*Cleans up messes, in love guides*

***Whetstone, p. 28 comparison is paraphrased.*

You may find that you are mature in some areas and in other areas you will need to rely on The Holy Spirit to grow you up. No matter what the case, you will need God's grace. Does this mean that God cannot use you? No! God can use any person who will yield to Him.

As the bones in our bodies have grown from infancy through maturity without any help from us, our spirit man doesn't need nor can we give it our physical help in hurrying up the process of Christ being manifested in our lives. It's only as we rest in Christ and cooperate with The Holy Spirit working in and through us that we will see the evidence of Jesus Christ manifested in our lives—not in our own strength, but in His. Then and only then will we grow in grace, grow in the knowledge of our Lord and Savior Jesus Christ, and be able to prove what is that good, and acceptable, and perfect Will of God.

Chapter 7
"Fruit—No Fruit, Fruit, More Fruit, Much Fruit"

Genesis 1:28 – "And God blessed them, and God said unto them, Be fruitful, and multiply, and replenish the earth, and subdue it: and have dominion over the fish of the sea, and over the fowl of the air, and over every living thing that moveth upon the earth."

    This has always been God's plan for us—To be fruitful, multiply, replenish the earth, subdue it, and have dominion. His plan has not changed! God created us and every living thing perfectly so that the very thing that would cause us to reproduce is in us—our reproductive organs, the seeds of apples, oranges, pears, watermelons, animals, birds, and every living thing! We were all told to be fruitful! But only man was told to subdue and dominate!

What God "said unto them" in Genesis 1:28 was before sin entered into the world. God was talking to His creation, man! Man had a spirit, made in the image of God, without sin and without any consciousness of sin. Because man was a spirit, *spiritual* children should have been birthed! But because of man's disobedience, sin entered in. Jesus came to redeem us back to God and He has placed His Word in our hearts and minds. Let's look at that Word as **_seed_** being placed into the fertile ground of our heart. Let's see how it reproduces.

The ground is prepared for the seed. The seed is planted. It is watered and nourished. Before you can see anything above the soil, it begins to open up in the ground. Then it sprouts, pushing through the soil, starts to grow all while care is given to it to see that it is well nourished. The seed is not disturbed. (Notice, we don't go back and dig up the seed to see if it's growing.) The seed gains nourishment and water from the soil around it. Care is given to make sure that no weeds grow up around it to steal its strength. As long as it stays in the ground, the fruit or plant continues to grow. The bud appears, the bloom bursts out, then the fruit!

As it grows, attached to the branches, vine, or stem, many times some of the branches and shoots have to be cut back in order to get the best fruit. Then it reaches maturity! We finally see the fruit! But no sooner is it removed from the branches, the fruit stops growing. Although the flesh or outer part of the fruit begins to decay or die once it is removed from the branch, that death is not the end. The ***many seeds*** within that fruit hold the potential for more fruit just like ***it*** if planted in good ground! Jesus is That Seed and He has been sown in the good ground of our hearts and minds!

Genesis 3:15 – *"And I will put enmity between thee and the woman, and between thy seed and <u>her seed</u>; it shall bruise thy head, and thou shalt bruise his heel."* Jesus is That Seed!

Galatians 3:16 (NKJV) – *"Now to Abraham and his Seed were the promises made. He does not say, "And to seeds," as of many, but as of one, "<u>And to your Seed," who is Christ</u>.*"

Again, That Seed, God's Word, Jesus, was sown in the good ground of our hearts and minds.

Jesus, **"The Seed,"** lived on earth, died, went into the ground, and resurrected from the grave that we might live! That Seed planted in us and watered by the Word, increases, resulting in other lives saved!

John 12:24-25 – *"Verily, verily, I say unto you, Except a corn of wheat fall into the ground and die, it abideth alone: but if it die, it bringeth forth much fruit. [25]He that loveth his life shall lose it; and he that hateth his life in this world shall keep it unto life eternal."*

Think about it. We must allow the outer flesh man to remain dead, crucified, so that the seed of God's Word in our spirit man can reproduce for God. The Apostle Paul said, and we now say, *"I am **crucified with Christ (dead)**: nevertheless I live; yet not I, but Christ lives in me: and **the life which I now live in the flesh I live by the faith of the Son of God**, Who loved me, and gave Himself for me"* (Galatians 2:20)!

Jesus said in **John 15:1** – *"I am the true vine, and my Father is the husbandman."*

Jesus is The True Vine, we are the branches and God our Father takes care of us! He is the Husbandman! Anything that is not like Him, He clips off so that we will produce more fruit!

Our main purpose on this earth is to bear fruit, to reproduce, subdue, and dominate! And by The Power of The Holy Ghost, we can subdue and dominate and take back everything the devil has stolen from us using the "weapons of our warfare" which are not carnal but mighty through God to the pulling down of strong holds!

Luke 8:15 – *"But that [seed] on the good ground are they, which in an honest and good heart, having heard the word, keep it, and bring forth fruit with patience."* **and, Mark 4:8** – *"And other fell on good ground, and did yield fruit that sprang up and increased; and brought forth, some thirty, and some sixty, and some an hundred."*

God's Word is the Seed that He has planted! Our hearts and minds are the **_good ground_** if we hear and keep His Word hidden in our hearts, meditating on It to do It! Be **_a doer_** of the Word and not just a hearer! We don't want hindrances to enter in! We don't want the cares of this life, deceitfulness of riches, offenses, etc. to uproot The Word so that It does not produce good fruit for the Kingdom of God! We can't do this in our own strength! We need the Power of The Holy Ghost in order to walk this Christian life! We need the Spirit of God working in and through us, to forever give us the willingness to do God's Good Pleasure!

Philippians 2:13 (NKJV) – _"for it is God who works in you both to will and to do for <u>His good pleasure</u>."_

Keep in mind that Jesus used parables in many instances to explain spiritual truths. In John 15:2-8 it mentions four degrees of fruit bearing—no fruit, fruit, more fruit, and much fruit. It's not talking about the fruit we eat. Neither is it talking about the fruit of The Spirit as found in Galatians 5:22-23, although abiding in Christ causes this fruit to mature. John 15:2-8 is talking about spiritual children!

Adam and Eve were made in the image of God. Because they were, the fruit of the Spirit was already in them. Therefore, Adam and Eve could have produced spiritual children just like they were. Their children would have been born without sin and born to live forever! When anyone accepts Jesus as Lord and Savior of their life, their sins are forgiven and they too are destined to live forever! This is what God wants for every person.

The Apostle Paul tells us in Ephesians 5:32 that the mystery he is talking about (in the preceding verses) has to do with Christ and the Church and he is using this example of a husband and wife coming together as one to show us how we are to submit to Him.

When we are one with Christ, totally submitted to Him, spiritual children are birthed into the Kingdom—souls are won to Christ (Ephesians 5:32). If we abide in The Word of God and let His Word abide in us, we will be fruitful and we will multiply!

When God told Adam and Eve to be fruitful, He was talking about spiritual children, made in His image! Guess what? Just as God expected spiritual children from Adam and Eve, God is still looking for spiritual children and He's expecting to use us to help birth them into the Kingdom of God for Him! We are laborers together with God (I Corinthians 3:9).

Jesus' love for His creation caused Him to come into this world to seek and to save those who were lost. He came here specifically to do the work that God The Father had sent Him to do—die for the sins of the whole world, past, present, and future sins forever and for all time! He did all this to bring us back into fellowship with The Father.

In Acts 1:8 it says that we would receive Power after The Holy Ghost is come on us to be witnesses for Him everywhere, even to the uttermost part of the earth! God wants spiritual children! He wants us to be about The Father's business and to reproduce! Every born-again believer is expected to be a soul winner! Proverbs 11:30b says, He who wins souls is wise!

John 4:35-36 – *"³⁵Say not ye, There are yet four months, and then cometh harvest? Behold, I say unto you, Lift up your eyes, and look on the fields; for they are white already to harvest. ³⁶And he that reapeth receiveth wages, and gathereth **fruit unto life eternal**: that both he that soweth and he that reapeth may rejoice together."*

This "harvest" that The Lord is talking about is a harvest of souls! The ***fruit*** is people! It's a "now" harvest, not "by and by." It is not God's desire that anyone would die and go to hell.

2 Peter 3:9 – *"The Lord is not slack concerning his promise, as some men count slackness; but is longsuffering to us-ward, not willing that any should perish, but that all should come to repentance."*

God wants what He wants from His people! He wants spiritual children birthed into The Kingdom of God!

In addition, did you know that the only place in the Word of God that promises **God will pay you wages**, **money**, for soul winning and that it is found in this Scripture?

John 4:36 – *"And he that reapeth <u>**receiveth wages**</u>, and <u>**gathereth fruit unto life eternal**</u>: that both he that soweth and he that reapeth may rejoice together."*

What is to be reaped are souls, souls gathered unto eternal life. What God orders, He is faithful to pay for! But don't think that you will get anything from God if your motives are not pure! He expects us to win souls for Him out of obedience to His Word and because of our genuine love for people! God looks on the heart and rewards us accordingly!

On "Bearing No Fruit"

John 15:2-4 – *"²Every branch in me that <u>beareth not fruit</u> he taketh away: and ever branch that <u>beareth fruit</u>, he purgeth [prunes] it, that it may bring forth <u>more fruit</u>. ³Now ye are clean through the word which I have spoken unto you. ⁴Abide in me, and I in you. As the branch cannot bear fruit of itself, except it abide in the vine; no more can ye, except ye abide in me."*

In John 15:2 Jesus says that every branch in Him that does not bear fruit He will take away and that the only way to bear fruit, to reproduce, is to abide in The Word, Jesus Christ!

John 15:2a – *"Every branch in me that <u>beareth not fruit</u> **he taketh away:**"* <u>**Jesus said this!**</u>

Some may say, "How can such a loving God do such a thing?" I will say this as The Word of God does:

Titus 2:11-12 – *"¹¹For the grace of God that bringeth salvation hath appeared to all men, ¹²Teaching us that, denying ungodliness and worldly lusts, we should live soberly, righteously, and godly in this present world."*

God's grace has been presented. It's up to the individual to accept God's grace. Have you ever had an experience where you did something you should not have done whether you knew it was wrong or not, only to have someone who does not profess salvation say to you that you should not have done that? The person saying that to you was not saved, but yet they knew that what you had done or said was wrong? That's because their ***consciousness*** of good and evil, right and wrong told them so. They ***knew*** it was wrong whether they had seen or heard it, and it's all because of Titus 2:11-12. God's grace had been presented to their conscience.

On bearing "no fruit," John 15:2a says that if no fruit is produced, God would take away those who bear ***no fruit!***

John 15:2-4 – *"Every branch in me that <u>beareth not fruit</u> he taketh away: and ever branch that <u>beareth fruit</u>, he purgeth [prunes] it, that it may bring forth <u>more fruit</u>. ³Now you are clean through the word which I have spoken unto you. ⁴Abide in me, and I in you. As the branch cannot bear fruit of itself, except it abide in the vine; no more can ye, except ye abide in me."*

Other verses that agree with what John 15:2a says are:

Romans 1:24, 26, 28, 32 – *"²⁴Wherefore <u>God also gave them up</u> through the lusts of their own hearts…²⁶For this cause <u>God gave them up</u> unto vile affections…²⁸And even as they did not like to retain God in their knowledge, <u>God gave them over</u> to a reprobate mind (morally corrupt and depraved)…³²Who knowing the judgement of God, that they which commit such things are worthy of death not only do the same, but have pleasure in them that do them."*

Romans 1:18-19 – *"¹⁸For the wrath of God is revealed from heaven against all ungodliness and unrighteousness of men, who hold the truth in unrighteousness; ¹⁹Because that which may be known of God is manifest in them; for God hath shown it unto them."*

Romans 1:18-32 deals with those who have heard The Word of God presented to them and received It, but decided not to retain It in their memory. In order for anyone to become ungodly or unrighteous, they have to have been godly or righteous at one time. Because this group of people did not want to retain or keep God in their knowledge, God gave them up, over to a reprobate mind (morally corrupt and depraved). They heard The Word but didn't want to keep The Word in their knowledge! So, God gave them up! God did it! Can God restore them? Yes!

The parables of the "Five Wise and Five Foolish Virgins," "Talents," and the "Sheep and Goats" found in Matthew 25 is another example of loss having been experienced. It is not our Father's desire that any should perish and that's why we have to be about our Father's business!

On "Bearing Fruit, More Fruit, Much Fruit

As we abide in Christ, we will reproduce! As we are washed with water by His Word, not conforming to this world but being transformed by the renewing of our minds with His Word and allowing The Spirit of God to do His Word through us, the world will see our good works and glorify The Father! They will see the Power of The Holy Spirit working in and through our lives!

__John 15:5, 7-8__ – "⁵I am the vine, ye are the branches: He that abideth in me, and I in him, the same bringeth forth <u>much fruit</u>: for without me ye can do nothing.... ⁷If ye abide in me, and my words abide in you, ye shall ask what ye will, and it shall be done unto you. ⁸Herein is my Father glorified, that ye bear <u>much fruit</u>; so shall ye be my disciples."

__I Corinthians 2:4__ – "And my speech and my preaching was not with enticing words of man's wisdom, but in __<u>demonstration of the Spirit and power:</u>__" That Power is the Holy Ghost Power!

Our Father knows all about us and His plans for us. He knows how He wants to use us. He gives "gifts" as He chooses to help us get the job done (Romans 12:5-8; I Corinthians 12:8-10; Ephesians 4:11)!

I may not be used by God to do what you are called to do, and you may not be used by God to do what I am called to do, but each gift is important! There are no "big I's" and "little you's" in God's Kingdom! No one should think that they are "less than" or "more than" another. When we compare ourselves with someone else, The Word of God says we are not wise and says we are carnal (2 Corinthians 10:12 and 1 Corinthians 3:3)! ***Souls***, and souls only are what God wants—not carnality!

2 Corinthians 10:12 – *"For we dare not make ourselves of the number, or compare ourselves with some that commend themselves: but they measuring themselves among themselves, are <u>not wise</u>."*

I Corinthians 3:3 – *"For ye are yet <u>carnal</u>: for whereas there is among you envying, and strife, and divisions, are ye not carnal, and walk as men?"*

You will find that as you abide in Him and let His Word abide in you, and as you are led by His Spirit within you, you will find yourself being used by God in ways you have never imagined and souls will be won into The Kingdom of God!

I Corinthians 3:7-9 – *"[7]So then neither is he that planteth any thing, neither he that watereth; but <u>God that giveth the increase</u>. [8]Now he that planteth and he that watereth are one: and every man* *shall receive <u>his own reward according to his own labour</u>. ⁹For we are labourers together with God: ye are God's husbandry, ye are God's building."*

God gets all the glory! He gives the increase! He causes His Body, His Church, to grow and we are members in His Body, laborers together with God!

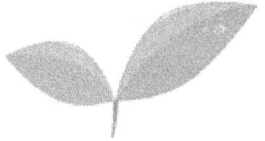

Chapter 8
"The Results"

The results of continuous spiritual growth and maturity is a sanctified life. This sanctified life, when led by The Spirit of God, produces spiritual children birthed into the Kingdom of God.

What does sanctification or to be sanctified mean? The dictionary states that to be sanctified means "to be set apart to a sacred purpose or to a religious use; to consecrate; to be free from sin; to purify." If we look at this definition through spiritual eyes, we see that to be sanctified means that we are cleaned up by The Spirit of God, which is The Word, and set aside for a specific work or use.

What are some of the things that The Word says about sanctification?

Sanctification is God's Will for us. *I Thessalonians 4:3 – "For this is the <u>will of God</u>, even your sanctification…"* In *John 17:17*, Jesus prays to The Father asking Him to, *"<u>Sanctify them through thy truth: thy word is truth.</u>"* In this last Scripture, Jesus is praying about us and for all those who will believe on Him as a result of our witness. He's praying that both would be sanctified by The Word of God.

Ephesians 5:26-27 – "²⁶That he might <u>sanctify and cleanse it</u> with the washing of water by the word. ²⁷That he might present it to himself a glorious church, not having spot, or wrinkle, or any such thing; but that it should be holy and without blemish."

I Thessalonians 5:23 – "And the very God of peace sanctify you wholly; and I pray God your whole spirit and soul and body be preserved blameless unto the coming of our Lord Jesus Christ."

John 17:18-20 - "¹⁸As thou hast sent me into the world, even so have I also sent them into the world. ¹⁹And for their sakes I sanctify myself, that they also might be <u>sanctified through the truth</u>. ²⁰Neither pray I for these alone, but for them also which shall believe on me through their word;"

God cleanses us from sin by the Blood of Jesus, continually washes the traces of sin out of our flesh by the Spirit with His

Word, and He sets us apart for His use. Jesus is coming back for a Church without a spot or wrinkle or any such thing! He's cleansing our flesh from anything that looks like a spot or a wrinkle!

When you know that your desire is to follow after the things of God and in your walk with Him get a tugging in your spirit man ***not to do*** something and you don't have Scripture for it, then that is an "any such thing" that God wants to keep us from (Ephesians 5:27). The Apostle Paul says if you have the mind to do anything other than to please God and pressing into the things of God, He will reveal it to you. Listen for the "still, small voice" on the inside of you. The Word tells us that those who are led by the Spirit of God are the sons of God!

Philippians 3:14-15 *– "[14]I press toward the mark for the prize of the high calling of God in Christ Jesus. [15]Let us therefore, as many as be perfect [mature], be thus minded: and if in any thing ye be otherwise minded, God shall reveal even this unto you."*

Romans 8:14 *– "For as many as are led by the Spirit of God, they are the sons of God."*

I Thessalonians 5:23 *– "And the very God of peace <u>sanctify you wholly</u>; and I pray God your whole <u>spirit</u> and <u>soul</u> and <u>body</u> be preserved blameless unto the coming of our Lord Jesus Christ."*

God's Will is that our spirit, our soul, and our body be cleaned up and set apart for His service! The **_whole_** spirit, soul, and body sanctified! He has purified **_our spirit (our spirit man)_**, He wants our **_soul (mind)_** transformed by His Word, and He wants **_our body (our flesh)_** by His Spirit, free from the dominance of sin!

Just as the man and woman become one on their wedding night, so God wants an intimate relationship with us. In the Old Testament, it's called, "knowing him or her" (I Samuel 1:19-20). In The New Testament, God wants us to "know Him" and to be so intimate with Him, knowing what He likes and dislikes, that we take on His Divine Nature.

***2 Peter 1:3-4** – "³According as his divine power hath given unto us all things that pertain unto life and godliness, **through the knowledge of him** that hath called us to glory [light] and virtue [moral excellence]: ⁴Whereby are given unto us exceeding great and precious promises: that by these ye might be **partakers of the divine nature**, having escaped the corruption that is in the world through lust."*

This is why we have been saved! God wants us just like Him! He wants our minds so renewed, our bodies so consecrated, so dedicated to Him that spiritual children are birthed into the Kingdom of God as we are led by His Spirit to:

***Matthew 28:19-20** – "¹⁹**Go ye** therefore, and teach all nations, baptizing them in the name of the Father, and of the Son, and of* the Holy Ghost: [20]Teaching them to observe all things whatsoever I have commanded you: and, lo, I am with you always, even unto the end of the world: Amen."

Mark 16:17-18 – "[17]And these signs shall follow <u>them that believe</u>; In my name shall they cast out devils; they shall speak with new tongues; [18]They shall take up serpents; and if they drink any deadly thing, it shall not hurt them; they shall lay hands on the sick, and they shall recover."

It is not God's desire that any person should perish, but that all should come to repentance (2 Peter 3:9).

John 15:7-8 – "[7]If ye <u>abide</u> in me, and my words abide in you, ye shall <u>ask</u> what ye will, and it shall be <u>done</u> unto you. [8]Herein is <u>my Father glorified</u>, that ye bear <u>much fruit</u>, so shall ye be <u>my disciples</u>."

I John 5:14-15 – "[14]And this is the confidence that we have in him, that, if <u>we ask</u> any thing <u>according to his will, he heareth us</u>: [15]And if we know that he hear us, whatsoever we ask, we know that <u>we have the petitions</u> that we desired of him"

2 Timothy 2:19-21 – "[19]Nevertheless the foundation of God standeth sure, having this seal, The Lord knoweth them that are his. And, let ever one that nameth the name of Christ <u>depart from iniquity</u>. [20] But in a great house there are not only vessels of gold and of silver, but also of wood and of earth; and some to honour, *and some to dishonor. ²¹If a man therefore purge himself from these, he shall <u>be a vessel unto honour, sanctified, and meet for the master's use, and prepared unto every good work.</u>"*

The "Message Bible" states verses 20-21 as:

"²⁰In a well-furnished kitchen there are not only crystal goblets and silver platters, but waste cans and compost buckets—some containers used to serve fine meals, others to take out the garbage. ²¹Become the kind of container God can use to present any and every kind of gift to his guests for their blessing."

Greater is He Who is in you than he that is in the world! You are more than a conqueror and can do all things through Christ Who strengthens you!

We are not an unregenerate, fleshly man never having accepted Jesus Christ as our Lord and Savior.

We don't want to be that carnal man, having accepted Jesus as Lord and Savior, escaping hell, but not living a victorious life. One who satisfies his fleshly desires, not pleasing God.

But, we are that spiritual man. One who loves God with all his heart, soul, mind, and strength. One who submits his whole body to The Lord, wanting to please Him in everything we say and do. One who wants to grow up in Him in all things (Ephesians 4:15).

God wants the same for us. He wants us mature! But He will not force maturity on us. He wants us fruitful! He wants children birthed into The Kingdom of God! He wants the same thing from us that He wanted from Adam. He wants us fruitful! He wants us to multiply! He wants us to subdue and dominate and replenish the earth!

Go and make disciples unto God! Be fruitful and multiply, and replenish the earth, subdue and dominate! Be blessed!

NOTES:

Mabel A. King

I'm Saved! So, What's Next?

WORKS CITED

Robbins, Dickie L. (2005). *No Sudden Change.* Bloomington: Author House.

Whetstone, Faye. (2002). *Growing Up Spiritually.* New Castle: Gary Whetstone Worldwide Ministries.

About the Author

    Mabel A. King loves The Lord and loves people. She is also a lover of children and as a result has six beautiful daughters, one handsome son, 24 grandchildren and 34 great grandchildren, in addition to the many spiritual children and "adopted children" at her job where she was employed as a teacher for 24 years before her retirement.

    Mabel A. King was called by God to be a Missionary and is presently a member of Life In Christ Ministries, Chester, Pennsylvania where she serves under the Pastorate of Bishop Dickie L. Robbins as a Prayer Minister, Altar Counselor, and Follow-up Ministry Head. She has also taught several classes: The Ministry of Teacher I and II, Growing Up Spiritually, and Learning How to Trust God all of which, with the help of The Holy Spirit, she developed.

Earlier, the call of God on her life led her from Chester and Life in Christ to Delaware where she served at Victory Christian Fellowship, New Castle, Delaware under the Pastorate of Dr. Gary V. Whetstone. While there she served as a Prayer Minister, a member of the Adult Choir, as part of the Neighborhood Evangelism Team, and as a part of the Gary Whetstone Worldwide Ministries Mission Team. She graduated from GWWM School of Biblical Studies. She was led to move to Maryland to help with Baltimore's Victory where she, while still under the Pastorate of Dr. Whetstone, taught the Mobilizing Believers Class, was a Praise and Worship Leader, Head of the Neighborhood Evangelism Team, assisted with the Audio Ministry, was Interim Overseer of the church there for a brief period, and held church services in her home.

While in Maryland, she was led to Living Word Family Church where she served under the leadership of Pastors Charles and Esther Bell, where she taught a Discipleship Class. There she designed a tract which has been distributed and used in several states. God brought her back to Chester and to Life In Christ Ministries.

"I was a welfare recipient on food stamps. I literally could not remember things from one day to the next because of the mental abuse I suffered. God led my children and me out of that situation. The Lord has blessed me to achieve much; graduated from college with honors, twice nominated and received the Who's Who Among America's Teachers Award, awarded the Pennsylvania Adult and Continuing Education Award, and self-published several books. But nothing compares with the fact that it was God Who picked me up and gave me a new lease on life when He saved me allowing me to work together with Him in The Ministry! I love Him and I will always give Him the praise and honor and glory for all that He has done for me!"

www.ingramcontent.com/pod-product-compliance
Lightning Source LLC
Chambersburg PA
CBHW071157090426
42736CB00012B/2363